THE KINGDOM CONCEPT COMPANY

BY

TONIA GODFREY

Copyright © 2014 by Tonia Godfrey

All rights reserved. No part of this publication may be reproduced, stored in a retrieval system, or transmitted in any form or by any means - electronic, mechanical, digital, photocopy, recording, or any other - except for brief quotations in printed reviews, without the prior permission of the publisher.

For permission requests, write to the publisher, addressed "Attention: Permissions Coordinator," at the address below:

Tonia Godfrey
3406 Glenmore Avenue
Cincinnati, OH 45211
www.zbmtwest.com

Except where otherwise indicated, all Scripture quotations in this book are taken from the New American Standard Bible Copyright © 1960, 1962, 1963, 1968, 1971, 1972, 1973, 1975, 1977

Kingdom Concept Company / Tonia Godfrey - 1st edition

Dedication

I would like to dedicate this book to my Lord & Savior, Jesus Christ. Without Your Gifts & Grace, this book would not exist.

To my Pastor, my best friend and loving husband Melvin. You have been graced to push me to achieve things that are always beyond what I imagine, thanks baby!

To my Grandma Doris for all the English corrections and spelling lessons, you are the writer in me today.

To my late Mother Sharon Gilbert and Aunt Arlene Singleton, you are not here to read this but you both have contributed more to this work than you will ever know! I'll tell you all about it when I get to heaven!

I love you all

Table of Contents

Introduction 7

Chapter One
Savior Business...13

Chapter Two
Kingdom Mindset..29

Chapter Three
Spirit Of Truth..39

Chapter Four
In The Beginning...49

Chapter Five
Trouble In Transition....................................69

Chapter Six
Greater Than You...79

INTRODUCTION

This book may not be filled with hundreds of pages, but it is certainly filled with years of wisdom and experience. Our life is a collection of our own personal experiences and discoveries. As we journey through life, some of these experiences have made us better and others have made us worse. The experiences that have a negative effect on our lives are the ones that cause us to proceed through life in fear, and fear is the greatest enemy to our self-discovery. Self-discovery is necessary for true fulfillment in this life. People who have never had the blessing of discovering who they truly are have missed out on a part of life that brings an amazing sense of fulfillment. This part of life cannot be compared to anything that finances can bring about alone.

This kind of fulfillment comes from knowing who you truly are. The true you. The you before the influence of experience. The you, that no one or nothing can ever change. This is the part of you that smiles at something beautiful. It could also be something that makes you sad. It's not the thing that is vogue or couture, but it is the most simple and silent part of you. The part of you that simply is. It's the part of you that is "effortless".

Our society is very influential when it comes to how we are taught to think and view the world around us. This influence is temporary and ever changing. Styles come and then they go. An afro was once beautiful, then it was abominable and now it's "cool" again. That's not because it was ever inherently wrong, it's simply an influence that society has on the way that we think. It is important that we learn how to clearly distinguish the difference between society's influence and the tried and true way to discover what is truth. Once you discover truth, your life will come into a much clearer focus. This focus will allow you to realize the true you, the truth that you were really born to experience.

Now, please don't misunderstand. Bad things do happen in life, but adversity can either make you a better person by learning from it, or it can destroy and distort the life that you were born to live. This often happens after years and years of pain. That pain can make us jaded, unable to ever hope for anything good to come our way. On the other hand, adversity can push us to champion a cause, to fight against the very thing that created our pain, in turn preventing others from experiencing the same hurt.

This vantage point has caused me to see a bigger picture in this life we live. Specifically when it comes to business. Knowing the truth about who I was always created to be and embracing the things that I was born to love has helped me to live a life that others envy. I'm quick to tell them, "If a life of freedom and Godly self discovery is a life that you want to live, God has provided all you need to live it."

I have ventured to write this book to help you get closer to the place that you want to be in business and most importantly, In GOD.

God Bless,

Tonia Godfrey

Chapter One

Savior Business

You may want to ask the question, "Why Save Your Business?" The definition of Salvation in its simplest form comes from the Greek word Soteria - which means deliverance, preservation and safety. Jesus saves your soul, which is made up of your mind, will and emotions. This true soul salvation should filter through to every part of your life, even your business.

Our very nature causes us to compartmentalize the things that we do. When we do this, we tend to lose many of the benefits that are a part of salvation because we leave them at church on Sunday, or we simply limit those benefits to a one-time experience. It is this line of thinking that I am seeking to dispel as you read this book.

As a believer, when I truly began to understand my gift of salvation, I realized that it influenced every area of my life. I began to look at the way I lived my life, and subsequently, I conducted myself at work and in business differently. I began looking at problems around me and instead of complaining about them, I started seeking the Lord for solutions. I mean, I have the solution living on the inside of me, right?

As I began to look to GOD, THE SOLUTION, for my solutions, "God Ideas" began to flood my heart. I mean, too many to fathom. This all came because I started looking to THE SOLUTION for the solutions to the world around me. Boy, did He give them. *"Wisdom is the principal thing, therefore get wisdom, and in all thy getting, get understanding.*" **Proverbs 4:7**. The word wisdom in this verse means "skill at war" but it is also defined as "wisdom in administration". Yeah, you read it, wisdom in administration. The Lord cares about your business affairs and has provided you with wisdom as a business administrator!

This book is yet another example of Jesus - THE SOLUTION, giving me a solution to the world around me. This is the premise behind Savior Business. We have been trying to live this life for long enough by our own will power & wisdom. Some of us may have already surrendered our will to the One who can make our crooked paths straight. Most of the time, when we realize or acknowledge that we have this need, it didn't originate from a problem at work. Your marriage could be on the rocks. Maybe your children are on a path of self-destruction and you feel that you had a part to play in it. You may be struggling with a drug or sex addiction. It could be any number of things and I can almost guarantee, it's not work related! The need for salvation, before all, is a personal one. And what are we taught to do with our personal life at work?

LEAVE IT AT HOME! And that is exactly what we tend to do with our salvation.

Ok, I don't mean that you don't go to work, a new creation. Your colleagues may wonder, "Hey, what's gotten into Pete? He's walking around like he's got a new lease on life!" It's true. You have. You probably want to shout through he whole office "I met my Savior and He is wonderful!" This isn't the part of your change at work that I'm talking about.

I am talking about the way that you were taught to underwrite files. There are policies and there are procedures. There is a certain kind of client profile that fits a particular program and there is one that does not. PERIOD. Or, "All these people do is call in and complain, all day long!"

> *"The LORD will make you the head and not the tail, and you only will be above, and you will not be underneath, if you listen to the commandments of the LORD your God, which I charge you today, to observe them carefully…"*
>
> **Deuteronomy 28:13**

Your shift doesn't change, simply because you have been saved, but the way that you look at the work that you do on your shift surely should!

When we begin to live our life and make decisions that are founded on principles that we find in the Word of God, we begin to see things from a different perspective or "vantage point". Perspective is a very powerful thing. Let's look at an example of perspective. You have a business tycoon like Warren Buffett and a single low-income mother with 3 children. Both want to buy a house. The desire is the same but the perspective of the people involved is vastly different. Warren Buffett concerns himself with nothing more than what he wants and how much he wants to pay for it. The single mother on the other hand has to wonder, how much she can afford, will they approve her for a loan, and will she have enough for a down payment. One enters the process as the head another enters the process as the tail.

If the scripture tells us that the LORD will make us the head and not the tail, then our vantage point should change after salvation occurs. Often times, this does not happen. We have saved employees, full of solutions, still seeing themselves as mere employees. Many of them are employers whose perspective never changed.

We need to start seeing our world from the vantage point of the "Kings Kids". After all, our God is King of Kings, right? He is Lord of all right? **Romans 8:15** tells us *"For you have not received a spirit of slavery leading to fear again, but you have received a spirit of adoption as sons by which we cry out, "Abba! Father!"* We have received a spirit of adoption! Our Daddy is the King of all kings. Do you carry yourself as a child of The King or are you walking the streets of His kingdom afraid to receive your benefits because you still don't quite believe that they are for you? My friend, I'm here to tell you today, these benefits are for you! The Kings Kids make the decisions, they do the hiring, the firing, the promoting, they decide the raises and they sign the checks. It's time for the children in the Kingdom of God to take our responsibility in leadership. The Kingdom of God truly is the answer, the truth and the light that this dying world of darkness needs RIGHT NOW! This takes discipline and this takes faith.

God has given us the following Kingdom Principle in **Romans 13:8** *"Owe nothing to anyone except to love one another; for he who loves his neighbor has fulfilled the law."*

In most cases, when you owe something or someone, there is a promise to repay that which you have borrowed. The instant you promise to repay something to someone, you have limited your freedom and flexibility to do only that which God is prompting you to. Let me give you an example. Let's say you are a salesperson at the local dealership. You have a very nice car that you're making payments on as well as a home with a mortgage payment. You have a few small credit cards, but not too much in the way of credit card debt. It's that day care that costs you so much! You have had a decent month so far just not quite enough to cover your obligations after you have paid the day care provider. You are now feeling the pressure to produce. You can't make this car payment late again, there are no more arrangements that you can make on the loan and this one will affect your credit score. That cannot happen because you and your wife have been discussing building a new house because the one you live in now is getting too small! So, here comes a customer in a fancy BMW getting out of with a beaming teenager. As soon as you stick out your hand to greet them you have the thought, I should introduce them to Sarah. But your lightning fast mind quickly does the math. You realize this deal could cover the rest of the mortgage and your car payment, so you proceed in your greeting. You begin to feel uneasiness with every vehicle that you show & you keep thinking that Sarah should really be the one working with them. You still dismiss that thought because heck, you've got a family & small mouths to feed! You finish the deal and pay your bills. The beginning of the next month, you notice that you haven't seen Sarah around the dealership. When you inquire, you find out that Sarah was let go because she had one final month to produce her quota. The messed up part is that she was 1 sale shy of her goal. Sarah has 2 young children and no financial support at home.

Do you see how it would have been much easier for this sales person to be sensitive to the prompting of the Lord had they not had so many financial obligations of their own?

People make these decisions and override the voice of God every single day. The power of owing money is strong and it directs the decisions of people all the time. From the kind of client you decide to work with, to whether or not you set out into your own business. When you have this kind of influence directing your decision making process you soon realize that you are NOT free to simply do, what God is directing you to do. Think about some of the decisions that you have made lately. Have any of them been influenced by what you owe or what you have already promised to pay?

You also have people who aren't free to give to their local church or charity because all of their paycheck has already been allocated to "bill money". And I mean all! Monthly payments are like greedy little monsters just waiting for your direct deposit to hit your bank account. Your paycheck did nothing more than keep those pesky phone calls quiet for another 30 days.

The Lord may have been prompting you to start giving your tithes again. Maybe because you have gotten away from it and haven't been free to trust Him with your finances for some years now. You receive yet another prompting, and all you can think is that you can't afford to. You may say, "I have made all of these promises to pay and they don't sit silently if I miss a payment like you do God." What God knows is this, He has an abundant harvest tied up in your tithes and He is requiring your simple act of faith to release it. That simple act of faith gives Him the authority to turn on His faucet of favor that will free you from this financial bondage. He already had a plan set in motion for you that would allow you to not only meet but also pay off those pesky obligations that resulted from impulsive decisions. Your Father sees that these obligations have become a heavy burden for you. Jesus tells us this: *"Come to Me, all who are weary and heavy-laden, and I will give you rest. Take My yoke upon you and learn from Me, for I am gentle and humble in heart, and you will find rest for your souls. For My yoke is easy and My burden is light."*-**Matthew 11:28-30.** I have never once had a bill collector tell me that! God wants to set you free and you have to pay back what you borrow. I call this the "debt dilemma"! If you find yourself making these kind of choices, it can be very difficult to follow the direction of the Lord when He prompts you to pursue a new business venture.

I believe that we have so many entrepreneurs in the Kingdom of God, who have been designed to be employers. The Kingdom of God should be the place where the hurting and jobless come to find help and hope for their future. But instead, these people find that the Kings Kids are still out working in the pigpen like the prodigal son. He wasn't free to help anyone while he was working in the muck, but as soon as he went home to his father, he was restored to his

FULL authority and dominion as a master in his father's kingdom.

God wants us to be able to pay our bills. We will always have utilities and basic responsibilities. The bills we acquire by choice and not because of true necessity are the ones that interfere with God's plans for us. It is the bills, which God never intended for us to originate, that have the potential to prevent God's children from being the solution that He designed us to be. Debt can be truly dangerous to the Kings Kids!

Debt freedom is a Kingdom Concept for a good reason.

Chapter Two

Kingdom Mindset

We have already started to address the importance of our mindset. In order to walk in the fullness of Savior Business, we must first understand that The Kings Kids operate under a totally different set of rules and guidelines. These rules don't exempt us from the laws placed on the rest of society, it actually means that we live our lives according to a higher standard. There is a greater expectation placed on us because of who our Father is. Remember, we have the spirit of adoption. One caveat is that if the laws given by society contradict the standards and values given by the King, I have a moral responsibility to honor my Father and King above all and before all. This is how a kingdom operates.

    The word Kingdom occurs 321 times in all of the Old Testament and 299 times in the New Testament. The Old Testament is 3.5 times longer than the New Testament so that says a lot about emphasis! If God is placing this kind of emphasis on Kingdom in the smallest portion of His love letter to us, the portion of His Word that gives us the most insight into how He desires for us to live our lives today, I think that we ought to pay attention! Hence, the revelation of the Kingdom Concept.

1 Corinthians 4:20 tells us that *"The Kingdom of God does not consist in words but in power."* Two of the most important things our Father the King has given to his children are power and authority. The Kingdom Mindset, is knowing that we have the authority to speak change, and having the power of the kingdom to back us up. It is one thing to declare, *"I am a child of the King."* It is another thing to declare, *"I am a child of the King"* and have the King declare, "This is my child." If you don't believe me, ask my Daddy! You have been given authority to use His

> *"God has chosen the foolish things of this world to shame the wise and, God has chosen the weak things of this world to shame the things which are strong."*
>
> **1 Corinthians 1:27**

name, the name of Jesus, our key to demonstration and power.

People will not understand why and how you are able to do the things that you do. It is because you are a child of the King and the favor of God rests upon you. You have been endowed with the Kings dominion and authority. When you are living in alignment with the Kings favor and ruler-ship, He moves mountains according to your word (as long as your words line up with His). He will open doors that no one can shut. You get all the backing of His army of angels just waiting for you to direct them according to the Word of the King, the Word of God.

> *"Bless the LORD, you His angels, mighty in strength, who perform His Word, obeying the voice of His Word!"*
>
> **Psalm 103:20**

God's angels obey the voice of His word! Who gives voice to His Word? His kids do, that's who!

Developing a Kingdom Mindset requires a paradigm shift. We transition from how we have been accustomed to living and thinking, to a new Kingdom way of living and thinking. This is where things may get a bit tricky. Take Prince William, born into his father's kingdom. He has been surrounded by royalty his whole life. He knows nothing different than life as a prince. Having the mindset of a prince requires little effort on his part because, after all his years of training, kingdom living happens automatically.

Princess Kate on the other hand, had to become royalty. In her first months as part of the family, I'm sure she had days when she felt that learning this way of life was difficult. She may have even had moments when she thought that she wouldn't measure up. But now we see a beautiful woman carrying herself just as if she had always been royalty. Kate Middleton had to change her mindset. Marrying Prince William made her a princess. She had to learn how to live like one, and she has!

Let's go back to **Romans 8:15** *"For you have not received a spirit of slavery leading to fear again, but you have received a spirit of adoption as sons by which we cry out, "Abba! Father!"*

Who would have a harder time adjusting to their new life when they were adopted? Would it be the 6 month old child or the 16 year old child? The 16 year old child would most definitely have a more difficult time adjusting to life and receiving the love from their new family. Why? The older child has had 16 years of a long hard life to unlearn and forget. Many of us have never forgotten the pain of our own troubled past. We may receive salvation and can even accept the forgiveness of our sins, but many still have trouble thinking like a child of the King while here living our life on earth. I don't know any one of us who has a beef with getting into heaven! However we have to learn how to think and act like the Kings young princes and princesses now! Often times, we reject this life because we don't feel we have done what it takes to deserve it. We continue to struggle as the commoners do according to our own power. Our Father loved us so much that He made the way for us because he knew that we never could!

So, how do we learn how to think like a child of the King?

> *"And do not be conformed to this world, but be transformed by the renewing of your mind, so that you may prove what the will of God is, that which is good and acceptable and perfect."*
>
> **Romans 12:2**

That's how. We **must** renew our minds by the Word of God, I cannot emphasize this enough, it is of the **utmost importance**! We must wash away our old way of thinking, being and doing. This will welcome a new way of thinking, which will lead to a new way of being, which will in turn create in us a new way of doing. How is this done? By reading, eating, meditating on and digesting regularly the Word of God! There is one way and one way only that will cause your thinking to undergo a lasting change. **Hebrews 4:12** tells us *"For the word of God is living and active and sharper than any two-edged* *sword, and piercing as far as the division of soul and spirit, of both joints and marrow, and able to judge the thoughts and intentions of the heart."* It will get you right down to it! If you need to change, it is the Word of God that will bring about the true change that you desire. It is the Word of our King that we believe and therefore speak or give voice to that will in turn give His angels something to obey. This is what will bring a true and lasting Kingdom Mindset to our lives.

CHAPTER THREE

SPIRIT OF TRUTH

"But when He, the Spirit of truth, comes, He will guide you into all the truth; for He will not speak on His own initiative, but whatever He hears, He will speak; and He will disclose to you what is to come.

John 16:13

The Spirit of Truth has a very important part to play in understanding the Kingdom that we now live in. Jesus told his disciples this: *"But I tell you the truth, it is to your advantage that I go away; for if I do not go away, the Helper will not come to you; but if I go, I will send Him to you."* **John 16:7.** It was to our advantage that Jesus sent His Holy Spirit back to us. What an advantage He has given! The Spirit of Truth was sent here to guide us into all truth. He doesn't speak on his own initiative. Whatever He hears the Father say is what He repeats to us. He will disclose to us the things that are to come.

Some people reserve the work of God's Holy Spirit to a one-time experience that was evidenced by them speaking in tongues. This gift is so important, but there is much more that His Holy Spirit has been sent to do. We have to know what to expect in order to allow Him to function in our lives.

> *Jesus answered and said to him, "If anyone loves Me, he will keep My word; and My Father will love him, and We will come to him and make Our abode with him."*
>
> **John 14:23**

What can be closer than living with someone? Living in them! And that is exactly what God did through the work of Jesus Christ and His mighty Holy Spirit! *"Do you not know that you are a temple of God and that the Spirit of God dwells in you?"* **1 Corinthians 3:16.** What an awesome Father and what an awesome gift! Remember **1 Corinthians 4:20** *"The Kingdom of God does not consist in words but in power."* The

Spirit of truth is who endues us with the power we need to operate as the Kings Kids!

He also supplies us with the power and ability we need to operate in our business and personal life successfully

> "but you will receive power when the Holy Spirit has come upon you; and you shall be My witnesses both in Jerusalem, and in all Judea and Samaria, and even to the remotest part of the earth."
> Acts 1:18

with the renewed mindset of the Kings Kids!

With a mind renewed by the Word of God, His Spirit of truth will cause you to understand things around you with the eyes of Christ. The Spirit of God will teach you how to see situations and challenges in life and business the way that

God sees them. He helps us the to see the "bigger picture".

My husband always says *"There are three sides to every story; your side, my side and the truth"*. Think about this. Have you ever been caught in the middle of a disagreement? How did you feel when person one told you what happened? Let's say that a couple of days pass before you hear the other person's side. In those two days, if you're not careful, you may begin forming an opinion about the other person involved. You and person two finally meet and they get to tell you what "really" happened. Well, sort of. They are actually giving you their side or perspective. Suddenly, they don't seem so wrong in the situation. Now you don't know what to think because of the conflicting stories. The truth, is somewhere mixed in the two. The only One who knows the truth is God. *"But just as it is written "Things that eye has not seen and ear has not heard and which has not entered the heart of man, all that, God has prepared for those who love Him. For to us God revealed them through the Spirit, for the Spirit searches all things even the depths of God. For who among men knows the thoughts of a man except the spirit of the man which is in him? Even so the thoughts of God no one knows except the Spirit of God. Now we have received, not the spirit of the world, but the Spirit who is from God, so that we may know the things freely given to us by God...*

1 Corinthians 2:11-12

Life, when we live it based solely on our five senses, usually only tells us one side of the story. When we make life or business decisions simply because of facts and reports, we limit ourselves to just one side of the story. There is always another side to the facts that we choose to believe. I think that we should believe in something greater than facts because facts are NOT truth. Facts change. Truth endures. This is why it is so important as children of the King to know the Truth. *"So Jesus was saying to the Jews who had believed Him "If you continue in my Word then you truly are disciples of Mine; and you will know the truth and the truth will make you free."* **John 8:31:32.** It is the truth that we KNOW that will make us free. Free from facts that fluctuate with the market and the economy!

It was once a fact that our economy was collapsing as a result of a failed real estate market. It is now a fact that the real estate market is rebounding and our economy stabilizing. The truth was, is and will always be this:

> *"And my God will supply all your needs according to His riches in glory in Christ Jesus."*
>
> **Philippians 4:19**

Knowing this truth gave me the confidence I needed to start my business. It is a business that was directly influenced by the real estate market. 2009 was the height of the "Mortgage Crisis". It is also the year I established my Real Estate Closing Agency. A closing doesn't happen until a house sells. You do the math. Some people would say that only a fool would start a closing agency when the facts are telling us that the real estate and mortgage industry are collapsing! Knowing the Truth gave me the freedom & confidence I needed to make that decision. That decision created a stream of provision God used to sustain my family during and after the "mortgage crisis."

If you haven't already, I pray that you are beginning to realize just how important it is to allow the Spirit of truth teach and guide you into all truth. The truth that concerns life as a whole and the truth about everything that specifically concerns you!

Chapter Four

In the Beginning

"In the beginning God created the heavens and the earth...Let Us make man in Our image, according to Our likeness..." Genesis 1:1,26

I believe that every part of me was made in God's image. I believe the Truth that says, *"In the beginning God created"*. The very first thing God did was to create. I believe we are created beings who, have been created to create. It is instinctual for us to want to pro-create. The bible calls it "being fruitful". There is a primal desire in mankind to become intimate with another in love. Out of that love, another unique individual is created. This is a tiny, beautiful, perfect person. A miraculous creation that looks, walks, talks and often times acts just like you. Where do you think this desire came from? *"Let Us make man in Our image"*, sound familiar? Children aren't the only thing that we were created to create.

In order for us to understand how to run our business according to biblical Kingdom Concepts and principles, we need to learn how to recognize and embrace the thing or things that God has created us to create. Every one of us is different. Each of us has a unique cocktail of gifts, talents and abilities within us.

One thing that helps us determine whether we are using our God given talents or simply doing a job is a sense of fulfillment, or lack thereof. I'm not talking about just doing something your good at. This is the kind of work that you find so fulfilling that you could easily do it for free! Even cooler is that when you do it, God, will cause favor to come your way and people will want to pay you for it! Quite handsomely I might add!

Fulfillment comes from the problems you are created to solve. The answer you are called to be!!! You don't need an alarm to wake up and do this work. You wake up in the middle of the night because your brain is constantly coming up with creative ways to do it better. It flows from the part that is God within you. This is how the company operating from the Kingdom Concept functions.

Now, lets talk about some hindrances to our creativity, because we all have them. First of all, life in general can be a hindrance to creativity. This starts when we allow the circumstances of every day living to keep us from spending personal time with God in His Word, and in His presence in prayer. This time is extremely important because it is in this time that we acknowledge our Heavenly Father as our source of direction and inspiration. It is here that we lay our burdens at His feet. It is here that we discover our solutions so that we know how to go back out into the world tomorrow and be the solution that our world around us needs us to be.

Debt and financial obligations are yet another stronghold that can stifle creativity. Worry results from financial stress. Worry hinders creativity because worry takes up space in our brain. When worry is leasing our brain space then creativity can't have it. Worry causes us to be double minded. *"Consider it all joy my brethren, when you encounter various trials, knowing that the testing of your faith produces endurance. And let endurance have its perfect result, so that you may be perfect and complete, lacking nothing. But if any of you lacks wisdom, let him ask of God who gives to all generously and without reproach, and it will be given to him. But he must ask in faith, without any doubting, for the one who doubts is like the surf of the sea, driven and tossed by the wind. For that man ought not to expect that he will receive anything from the Lord, being a double minded man, unstable in all his ways."* **James 1:2-8.**

I don't know if you have ever put in a relaxer. But the cream has a chemical in it that straightens coarse hair. If left in too long it can cause burns to the scalp and could eventually even dissolve away the hair. Once the hair has reached the desired straightness, the professional will apply what is called a neutralizing shampoo. They wash out the cream with this special shampoo because it neutralizes the relaxer causing it to stop working. Much in the same way, worry neutralizes creativity. This is why understanding how to operate our lives and businesses according to principles of faith is so important. Believing in the truth *that we know* is also important. The truth *that we know* keeps us from being double minded. Mounting debt and financial obligations cause worry. Worry contradicts faith, which in turn will neutralize our creativity.

It is important that we allow our creativity to remain intact, so that the plan of God is free to be fulfilled in our lives. Goodness gracious, please don't create any unnecessary blockages for yourself because of yourself! Dang! Dang! Dang! It's like I can see our enemy grabbing our hand, balling it up into a fist and punching us in the face with our own hand, saying "Why do you keep hitting yourself, why do you keep hitting yourself!?!?" Stop it, please, just stop it! We drop our weapon, and in an effort to save ourselves we reach in our pocket and throw the bullets at him. Like that's gonna hurt... Then, we have the nerve to be pissed off and blame God because satan picks up our gun, loads the bullets and shoots us in the back all while we're busy running away from him screaming & crying, pouting & complaining. That makes absolutely no sense does it? How do you think that God feels!?!

Lifestyle, comfort zone and standard of living can all be great hindrances to our creativity. Lifestyle is the typical way of life of an individual, group, or culture. Here is an example. Lets take a $1,700/month mortgage payment. For some people that $1,700 a month may sound like a shack. For me, it is simply a comfortable living. A comfort zone is a behavioral state within which a person operates in an anxiety-neutral condition, using a limited set of behaviors to deliver a steady level of performance, usually without a sense of risk. i.e. *"I ain't quitting my job."* All while your boss stresses you out so much that you recently received a high blood pressure diagnosis! Standard of living refers to the level of wealth, comfort, material goods and necessities available to a certain socioeconomic class. Ever heard these: *'Oh, noooo! I could NEVER buy a used car!'* Or, *'A $100,000 house would be a match box for my family!'*, *'But, I won't be able to go shopping and wear the latest designer fashions.'* These are vicious cycles.

The more you make, the more your borrow, the more you borrow, the more you owe, the more you owe, the more you have to repay, the more you have to repay, the deeper into the clutches of death, oh, I mean debt you go! I wish you could see my face... The influence that social status has on our financial decisions is sickening. So many of us never realize just how much this directly influences our faith. It makes us choose between doing what God wants us to, or what our finances tell us to, but we cannot do both. I have to say it... because the Bible does...

> *"No one can serve two masters; for either he will hate the one and love the other, or he will be devoted to one and despise the other. You cannot serve God and wealth."*
> **Mathew 6:26.**

The Word of God doesn't say this stuff just to sound deep. Life is serious! God sent Jesus - The Living Word - to shine His light on those dark places that have hindered His children from realizing the fullness of the benefits of their adoption for far too long! *"In the beginning was the Word and the Word was with God and the Word was God. He was in the beginning with God. All things came into being through Him, and apart from Him nothing came into being that has come into being. In Him was the life and the life was the Light of men. The Light shines in the darkness, and the darkness did not comprehend it."* **John 1:1-5.** The Word knew that we would need the Light and the Light would be the life that we need in our world!

It's time that we let the light of the Word of God shine on those dark places in our life and business. It's time we learn how to release our God given creativity into the places that have been held hostage by social expectations and self-sabotage. It's time to tell hindrances to go, go, go, and your God given creativity to flow, flow, flow!

Before we continue reading lets pause for a moment and activate what we have received thus far. If you agree with me, we should take this time to straighten out some things in prayer. There are at least 3. Please pray all and specifically the ones that are needed for your life.

Prayer of acknowledgement:

Father, In the Name of Jesus,

I thank you that I have been created in Your image. Thank you for the gifts and talents that you have placed on the inside of me. Father, I thank you for creating such an awesome plan of salvation for my life and also for my business. If there is any area of my life that I am not exercising the fullness of the Kingdom authority that You supplied for me, I ask that You reveal those places to me and I ask

You to guide me into the truth about Your will for my life and business. I also ask that you forgive me for the things in my life I have done, or decisions I have made that have created situations that prevented me from experiencing the fullness of Your Kingdom grace and favor. I thank You for guiding me through and out of the dark places of my life and into Your marvelous light. All this I ask and receive as done, In the Name of Jesus, Amen.

Prayer of Salvation:

Father, In the Name of Jesus, I thank You for creating such a great plan for salvation. I believe that You died so that I can live in You. I also believe that God raised You from the dead, so that I no longer have to die as a result of the sin and misdeeds of my life. Father, I acknowledge that I have made some big mistakes. I also recognize that I am not walking in the fullness of the calling that You have for my life. I recognize my need for a Savior. I ask that You forgive me for my sins. Every decision, every action, and every thought that was or is not like You, please help me stay away from these actions, behaviors and decisions since they displease You. I don't want my relationship with You to be hindered another day! I cannot live this life without You. I want to live my life from this day forward because of You. Not my will, but Father, let Your will be done in me and through me. I thank You, that I am forgiven. I thank You, that I am saved. I thank You that I am now one of Yours, and I receive my place in Your Kingdom. You are now LORD of my life and I recognize you as LORD of all. Now. In Jesus Name, Amen!

"If you confess with your mouth Jesus as Lord, and believe in your heart that God raised Him from the dead, you will be saved. For with the heart a person believes, and with the mouth he confesses, resulting in salvation.

Romans 10:9-10

Prayer to receive the Holy Spirit:

Let me begin by saying this. The bible refers to this as receiving the gift of the Holy Spirit. Salvation and receiving the gift of the Holy Spirit are two separate experiences and baptism is yet another. If you haven't already, I would encourage you to find a Bible believing church home, a place where you can be baptized **in the Name of Jesus**.

There is something about that Name. Pay close attention to society around you. It's subtle but it's definitely there. People don't want to say His name. Why, you may wonder? There is just something about that name! At the name of JESUS, demons tremble! There is Power in the Name of Jesus! There is healing in the name of Jesus! There is deliverance in the name of Jesus! The Name of the Father, of the Son and of the Holy Ghost is His name. The Three are One. No

> *Jesus said to him, "I am the way, and the truth, and the life; no one comes to the Father but through Me.*
> **John 14:6**

one can come to the Father except through the Son. His name is JESUS! SO, SAY HIS NAME! Ask them (or yourself) next time, why didn't I say His name???????? Don't let society take your Savior's Name away from you! He gave it to you. It belongs to you. It is your right to use it. So use it! The Trump children aren't afraid to use their name, neither are the Kardashians. Benefits and blessing come with His Name. Don't let society trick you into staying "in the closet" and not receiving all of the benefits that come from using the Name of Jesus! His name identifies. Don't be ashamed to use it! *For whoever is ashamed of Me and My words in this adulterous and sinful generation, the Son of Man will also be ashamed of him when He comes in the glory of His Father with the holy angels."*

Mark 8:38. ijs... (text speak for I'm just saying...)

Whew, anyway, receiving the Holy Spirit is the same as receiving a gift. There is no tarrying or waiting long hard stressful years needed to receive His Gift. Our Father is a good Dad and does not give terrible gifts, so receive ye the gift of the Holy Spirit.

Or what man is there among you who, when his son asks for a loaf, will give him a stone? Or if he asks for a fish, he will not give him a snake, will he? If you then, being evil, know how to give good gifts to your children, how much more will your Father who is in heaven give what is good to those who ask Him!

Matthew 7:9-11

Peter said to them, "Repent, and each of you be baptized in the name of Jesus Christ for the forgiveness of your sins; and you will receive the gift of the Holy Spirit.

Acts 2:38

Lets Pray:

Father, In the Name of Jesus, again, I thank You for your awesome plan of Salvation. I thank You that I was a sinner, in need of a Savior, and You became my Salvation. I thank You that You have a awesome plan for my life, a plan that I cannot fulfill according to my own power and ability. Father, I thank You that You have provided the power to help me be all that You have called me to be. I thank You that it was to my advantage that You went away and now Your Holy Spirit has been sent to come live in me. Right now Father I ask that You fill me with Your Holy Spirit. You said that If I ask for a loaf of bread, that You would not give me a stone, so I thank You that I do not have to fear receiving a counterfeit spirit or a stone. You created this gift and You know how to give Him to me. So, I receive your Holy Spirit. I thank You for filling me this day, In Jesus Name, Amen.

Now, breathe in a deep breath. This is activating your faith and breathing in the pneuma or the breath of Life, the Breath of His Holy Spirit.

Don't be surprised if you start speaking in an unknown tongue. It's biblical. You should, regularly. Read the Book of Acts please. This is a whole other subject pertinent to your success. Needless to say, it is an excellent practice in the development of our relationship with our Father as a Kings Kid! You are filled. You have been empowered and now you are equipped to do everything that God has created you to do, the way that He designed you to do it!

Chapter Five

Trouble in Transition

The Gospel of the Kingdom of God is also known as the "Good News". Some have even gone as far as to say that it is the "Too good to be true News". I agree. The news of the Gospel of Jesus Christ and what He has done for us is so good, that it is hard for many folks to believe and receive. That doesn't make it any less true. In this chapter, though, I want to share with you the realness. We think that reality TV is real. No, life is what's really real. It is only fitting that I address a misconception regarding our newfound life in Christ Jesus.

When people receive salvation, they walk away from the experience feeling ten feet tall! All of a sudden they can see more clearly and want to change the world! You believe that you can, because now, the One who can is living in you! This is all true.

When you receive salvation, your spirit, the eternal part of you is changed in an instant! Again, mankind was created in the image of God. We are a three part being. We are a spirit, who possesses a soul and lives in a body. Our soul also known as our psyche is the seat of our mind (the way we think), our will (the things we do), and our emotions (the way we feel). This part of us is NOT changed the instant that we are saved. This is the part of us that has been our "guiding light" up to this point in our lives and can be rather difficult to unseat. Ever heard the saying, "you can't teach an old dog new tricks"? It's a lot like that! Our soul is the reason that I put so much emphasis on renewing our minds by the Word of God in the previous chapter.

The good news of Salvation is great. Often times we walk away from our initial conversion with a misconceived notion that the seas of our troubled life are going to part and everything that we experience going forward will be on flat and dry ground. We think there will only be blue skies with no chance of showers or thunderstorms. Nope. Not happening.

Upon Salvation, the first thing that we need to learn how to do is renew our minds! We need to learn a new way of thinking. We need to learn a new manner of taking action and we need to learn a new way to feel about the situations that are constantly happening around us. Remember the Kingdom example. Don't get overwhelmed or worried. God gave us a solution for this too. It is His Word. Here's where you have a part to play! Remember that it is the *truth that you know*, that will set you free! The only way that you will know what is truth, and transform your thinking is by READING YOUR BIBLE! If you don't, your old ways of being, thinking, feeling and doing will continue to control your life and rob you of the Truth that God has for you!

Don't get discouraged if every business deal that comes your way now has some kind of problem. In the beginning, you should come to expect it. However, it should not stay this way! I say this because we have an adversary, the devil, who comes to *"...steal, kill and destroy..."* **John 10:10**. Our adversary, the devil, is on the prowl! **1 Peter 5:8** tells us *"Be of sober spirit, be on the alert. Your adversary, the devil, prowls around like a roaring lion, seeking someone to devour."* Did you notice that it says that the devil prowls around "like" a roaring lion. It never said that he is a roaring lion. He is a roaring "liar" but if he can get you to believe his lies, then he has accomplished his mission. Our adversary wants us to believe that our experience isn't real and that nothing has changed. He will try to convince you that you aren't saved. You haven't really received the Holy Spirit, and that your gift of tongues wasn't real. He will say that you just made that up. Lies, all lies! He is going about seeking to devour all that God has just transformed in your spirit, by bombarding your soul (mind, will & emotions) with lies that come through your five senses.

We have to learn how to live this life by letting our spirit lead. *"God is spirit, and those who worship Him must worship in spirit and truth."* **John 4:24.** When you begin to learn how to live your life and conduct your business through your spirit by being led by the Spirit of God that dwells in you, situations and circumstances that happen around you won't affect you the same way. You won't fly off the handle in a panic because you quickly realize and spiritually appraise that this situation is not truth and is subject to change. You acknowledge that this circumstance is subject to the Word of God and in the Name of Jesus, you declare the Truth of the Word of God regarding your situation. Then you rest. The devil cannot devour a person in this mind condition. They have put their mind, will and emotions in the back seat and have given their spirit, under the direction of the Holy Spirit, permission to drive their life. He quickly recognizes that he cannot devour you so he will go on to the next and try his tactics again. Don't think that he won't try and try again to deceive you. You must know you always have the victory because: *"...greater is He who is in you than he who is in the world."* **1 John 4:4.** Please remove this statement from your vocabulary, "The devil's been busy! He's been real busy!" You know what, if the devil had been busy, then God has been busier! Glorify the One that has made you great!

Don't worry. You will experience a change. You will experience the change as you begin to change. This isn't a change that is comprised of works. This is a change that comes only by the grace of God. Not the patty cake definition for grace that simply means unmerited favor. But the grace of God that literally empowers you with the ability to do what you could not according to your own power. God's grace literally gives you the things that you don't deserve and His mercy doesn't impart the judgment to you that you do! God's grace is a wonderful thing. It is awesome when you learn how to receive and walk in it to the Glory of God for you life and your business!

> *For by grace you have been saved through faith; and that not of yourselves, it is the gift of God; not as a result of works, so that no one may boast. For we are His workmanship, created in Christ Jesus for good works, which God prepared beforehand so that we would walk in them.*
>
> **Ephesians 2:8-10**

Walk in those good works, which God has prepared for you for His Glory, by His Grace!

Chapter Six
Greater Than You

This thing is so much greater than you.

The decisions that you make when it comes to your business go so much further than money ever could. It is much more than what you think that you can "afford to do". The sensitivity to your abilities and the decisions you make concerning them are directly related to the destiny of so many generations who will come after you. Godly wealth is from God.

> *"But you shall remember the Lord your God, for it is He who is giving you power to make wealth, that He may confirm His covenant which He swore to your fathers, as it is this day."*
> **Deuteronomy 8:18**

Wealth gotten by God is good. Wealth gotten to consume on our own lust is bad. *"You ask and do not receive, because you ask amiss, that you may spend it on your pleasures."* **James 4:3.** Watch out for this one. I have another book coming on that topic.

It is important to understand that our gifts and talents become skills as we perfect them by exercising them diligently. These skills, once mastered, can be taught to someone else. This new skill set has the potential to change the course of your life and someone else's life for generations to come! You have the ability to create an opportunity where there once was none.

I heard it said that the best public assistance is a job. I understood the sentiment, but a mere job is extremely limiting. I believe that the best kind of public assistance is a skill. A skill can be learned and turned into anything that you have the vision and ingenuity to develop it into. You can use a skill to get a job. You can use a skill to do a job. Or, you can use that same skill to start a business.

Once you've learned a skill, you have it and no one can take it away from you.

As entrepreneurs and business owners we have the opportunity to create jobs and develop skills. These skills will change lives all because you decided to pursue a dream!

I want to leave you with this. God has given us all talents and abilities. It is up to us to choose how we use them. If we are to lead successful lives and develop a business that has the substance necessary to transcend time and generations, we must learn how to let the Lord lead our in lives and business. Become a Kingdom Entrepreneur! Change the world around you with the gifts that are on the inside of you!

I want to talk about our children. How many of you ever wanted to do what your parents did when you grew up. Many children grow up and end up doing exactly the same kind of work that they saw their parents do. The really cool thing about it is, when this happens, it's usually because they want to and it becomes extremely fulfilling to the children too!

Here's a real life example. My father-in-law has been a pastor for over 40 years. His younger brother has been a pastor even longer. Today, both my husband and his first cousin are pastoring. They are both following in the footsteps of their fathers and are both truly fulfilled and love the work that they do. This doesn't just happen in church. Look at the Cake Boss! It could be a butcher, a doctor, a lawyer, a teacher, an architect or any other number of things.

That's the positive scenario. However, some children grow up to be what they see, and hate it. It's not gratifying or satisfying. It can be very painful. Have you ever wondered why there are generations of families living in subsidized housing & depending on the government for their survival? There are generations upon generations of living the same way. It is the path of least resistance that most people tend to follow.

Generally speaking, unless you encounter a life changer, someone or something who introduces you to a way of life different than your own, you may never veer off the path your currently walking. The opportunity to experience change may elude you. As my husband always so eloquently states, *"You don't know what you don't know!"* You may be the only entrepreneur in your family, or the first person to go to college. Because of you, those coming after you will always know that it can be done.

My Uncle did that for me. I had plenty of college graduates in my family. My mother didn't believe she could send me to college because of her lack of financial provision. God saw it differently. He used my uncle to tell her differently. He told my mom that I could, and you know what, I did. He went before me and the very thing I saw him do, I did too! He took an interest in my success & I did it!

Long before ever considering college, my Aunt Arlene became a licensed Nail Technician. I was her hand model when she took her state-board licensing exam. She lived in Michigan. My sister, brother and I would visit our family there every summer. Aunt Arlene taught me how to do nails. She would let me play on her front porch for hours upon hours in her "nail stuff". I got really good at it! Back home, I was getting a little reputation for my "nail art". I started out on myself, next my sister, and eventually all of the little girls at school wanted nail art too! My mom would get home from work there would be a trail of little girls leaving our house. I guess she noticed a pattern, because one day she told me, "If you're gonna have all these girls coming over here getting their nails done, you need to start charging!" I did, they paid, and that day, an entrepreneur was born.

My mother had the foresight to know that I would need a trade if I was going away to school. She recognized she wasn't able to send me away with my own car and monthly stipend; let alone tuition, room & board. She instructed me to save the money I would receive from family and friends upon my High School Graduation. In her wisdom, she had me use that money to enroll in a Nail Technician Licensing program at the local beauty college. That summer, my mom walked to work every day. She sacrificed the convenience of having a car, so that I could have transportation to beauty school in order to give me a means to obtain my nail license in the fall. I love, love, love her for that. The longer I live, the more I recognize the role that my Mothers foresight and sacrifice still has in my life. Both my Mother and my Aunt Arlene have since gone on to be with the Lord & I miss them dearly. They were both very important to me, so you can imagine the void that I still feel. That void is what this work is helping to heal.

Today, I cannot tell my mother or my aunt, therefore, I have made it my mission to tell the rest of the world that you can make a difference in your children's life! When you identify a gift, a gift that your children initiate an interest in, whenever possible, let them use it! Encourage them in it! Teach them the monetary value of it and let it help them in their life. It's a lot like when my dad taught me how to ride my bike. My Aunt & my Mom got me started, & I rode off on my own. Family can do that! You can do that! Family or not, you can make a difference!

I recognize that some of these matters are weighty. This is why I decided to start business coaching. My motto is simple, "Transform you, Transform your Business." *"For though by this time you ought to be teachers, you need someone to teach you again the first principles of the oracles of God; and you have come to need milk and not solid food. For everyone who partakes only of milk is unskilled in the word of righteousness, for he is a babe. But solid food belongs to those who are of full age, that is, those who by reason of use have their senses exercised to discern both good and evil."* **Hebrews 5:12-14.** The principles set forth in this book do not represent a simple one time "good read" but they have been written to hopefully set your life on a course of new decision making.

It's nice to have someone to walking this journey with you. Everyone needs someone to believe in their vision, goal and dreams.

It is awesome when you can share your life and business journey with your Pastor, but sometimes, if your pastor is not an entrepreneur, in certain areas of your business, it may be hard for them to relate. That's why I jokingly took the title of a *Pastorpreneur*. I quickly realized that this was not a joke. It is real. I believe that I have been uniquely positioned by God to have the heart of a Pastor with the mindset of an entrepreneur. I just get it. But I only get it by the grace of God. I don't separate or compartmentalize my spiritual life and my work life. They are who I am, so I function freely in both. This way of life and business may not be for you. I know that it is for someone because I exist. I love to see people discovering their gifts and talents and I get even more jazzed when a gift discovery becomes a life provision that brings a lifetime of fulfillment and joy.

My husband and I pastor a church that we believe will soon be full of what we call "Kingdom Entrepreneurs". Kingdom Entrepreneurs are bunch of great people who have set out to be the answer to the world's current "job crisis". It's time for the church be the answer again! It's time we stop being part of the problem and become the solution! Everyone needs help sometime, I just don't believe that God's children should have to go to everyone around us for help simply because our Kingdom brothers & sisters aren't in a position to help us in our need. The Kings Kids should instead be supplying the needs of everyone around us!

If you believe that, lets make some choices that will change the world! Remember, what you do is greater than you. It's like a ripple effect going down through time. Let's do our part to make a difference and leave our mark as Kings Kids on earth. We only have one life to live here, one life to learn and one life to love, so, let's make it count!

Resources:

If you would like to know more about becoming a Kingdom Entrepreneur or would like to discuss business coaching options with Tonia please visit:

www.zbmtwest.com

or

www.facebook.com/ToniaGodfrey

@ToniaGodfrey - Twitter

toniargodfrey@gmail.com

www.ingramcontent.com/pod-product-compliance
Lightning Source LLC
Chambersburg PA
CBHW071723170526
45165CB00005B/2134